Boise State University Western Writers Series   Number 64

Barry Lopez

By Peter Wild

University of Arizona

Editors: Wayne Chatterton
James H. Maguire

Business Manager:
James Hadden

Cover Design and Illustration
by Arny Skov, Copyright 1984

Boise State University, Boise, Idaho

Library of Congress Card No. 84-70252

International Standard Book No. 0-88430-038-2

Printed in the United States of America by
Boise State University Printing and Graphics Services
Boise, Idaho

Barry Lopez

Barry Lopez

In 1685, the people of Ansbach, Germany, chased a wolf. After finally killing it, they dressed the dead animal as a man, fixed a human mask to the carcass, then strung it up in the town square. Two hundred and ninety years later, Edward Abbey, a part-time forest ranger, writer, and self-styled hermit, wrote *The Monkey Wrench Gang* (Philadelphia: J. B. Lippincott, 1975). In his picaresque novel, a merry band of malcontents roars over the mountains and through the canyons of the American Southwest on midnight forays. They burn down signs advertising real estate and pour Karo syrup into the bowels of bulldozers.

At first thought, the two situations do not seem related—the one a rather bizarre occurrence in southern Germany of centuries ago, the other yet another emotion-filled, tongue-in-cheek publication by a best-selling writer—until one considers the contexts. As to the villagers of Ansbach, up until quite recently fear dominated people's attitudes toward wild nature. And with good reason, for nature in fact was man's antagonist. Unpredictable freezes, droughts, and floods ruined crops and threatened starvation. In the uncharted darkness of forests lurked not only human robbers and bears with dubious intentions toward humans, but, so it was thought, fiendish spirits eager to snatch up the unwary traveler body and soul. According to the wisdom of the day, the Devil himself used animals as agents of his mischief.

With this in mind, no wonder the German peasants rejoiced

around the wolf looking out with a human face in the square of Ansbach. They believed that they had slain a recently dead and unpopular mayor. In cahoots with Satan, he had come back to do them further injustice as a murderer of children and livestock. In such an atmosphere, hangings, even trials, of animals suspected of collusion with evil were not uncommon. Driven by feelings of helplessness, men projected their fears outward onto the natural world.

The public which now chuckles over the escapades of the rascals in *The Monkey Wrench Gang* considers the world in far different terms. No freezes, floods, or droughts threaten the ample food supply down at the local Safeway store. No wolves prowl howling around their condominiums at night. Now concerned citizens urge that the government preserve not only the nation's few remaining patches of wilderness but also, in contrast to the ignorant villagers of Ansbach, that it protect the few besieged wolves hiding in them. With this as a present-day backdrop, it is no surprise that readers clap with vicarious pleasure as Abbey's scallywag ecoraiders sabotage the tools of "progress," the instruments of nature's destruction. As Barry Lopez ponders the sudden change: "I write now in a country and at a time when man's own brutal nature is cause for concern and when the wolf, whom man has historically accused of craven savagery, has begun to emerge as a benign creature" (*Of Wolves and Men*, p. 73). In brief, nature the villain has become nature the hero. Yet as we shall see, several notes of irony, if not of disturbing contradiction, lie embedded in Lopez's observation.

Riding on the tide of public enthusiasm for nature, Barry Lopez has been compared variously to Carlos Castañeda, Loren Eiseley, John McPhee, Thoreau, Edward Abbey, Annie Dillard, Montaigne, even to Norman Mailer. He thus enjoys a stature incapable of fulfillment by any one human. Almost unanimously, reviewers have effused over Lopez's books, pointing to their "jewel-like prose," lauding their "magical, stunning similes," proclaiming the writing "a work of genius." Publication of *Of Wolves and Men* brought the retiring resident of Finn Rock, Oregon, somewhat bewildered into the lights of national television. Much of the praise is justified, some is not, but the point is this: amidst the favorable furor almost no one has taken the care to look deeply at Lopez's works and offer the more substantial compliment of a deeply-considered evaluation. That is, critics have tended to be dazzled by the surface of Lopez's writing.

Currently in demand as a speaker at the nation's most prestigious universities, soft-spoken Barry Lopez spends several months out of each year lecturing on the delicate esthetics of the Arctic, on the moral ambiguities of killing seals for scientific study. He chooses his words carefully and feels somewhat embarrassed when the audience's attention on him becomes "almost a physical thing, every heart in the room seeming to beat in time with his own" (Clarus Backes, "A Beer with a Writer of Feeling," p. 23). Hence, Lopez devotees may be surprised to find the author's earliest work in old copies of *Popular Science*. "What You Need to Know before You Buy 4-Wheel Drive" (March 1971, pp. 76-77, 137); "New Power Winches Wind up Your Work Quicker" (April 1974, pp. 108-110, 160); and "Learn from the Pros: How to Fell a Tree," (November 1974, pp. 112-13, 137) hardly seem likely beginnings for an author who today gives thanks for the intellectual rigors of sweating through the strict curriculum of a Jesuit high school, who looks to Gerard Manley Hopkins, William Faulkner, and James Agee as his creative mentors. Straightforward, unembellished, how-to pieces written for the avid handyman, the *Popular Science* articles reveal little of the future author dubbed "metaphysical" by a science writer for the *New York Times Book Review* (Bayard Webster, "A Bad

Press," p. 44). But the early writing did give the author-photographer confidence, a start in publishing, and a little money. As Lopez reflects on the period, "I was . . . making ends meet" (Letter from Lopez, 20 December 1982). As we shall see, the journalistic background, however, gave direction to his later work.

One might also consider the enduring freight of Lopez's Jesuitical education, for dualism typifies his writing. In it we see the dreamer and the realist, the scientist and the fabulist, the romantic and the classicist, white and Native American, the past and the present, refinement and a yen for primitivism vying over the years. At last, as Lopez approaches middle age, the forces have come into an exquisite balance.

A vignette in Tom Robbins' *Another Roadside Attraction* offers a clue to the nature of this equipoise. A wistful Amanda interrupts an old Navajo stooped over his sand painting. "What is the function of the artist?" she softly demands. Not at all nonplussed by the enticing busybody, the Indian informs her that "The function of the artist is to provide what life does not" (Garden City, New York: Doubleday, 1971, p. 19). One might also consider the bon mot in reverse, that life gives us what art does not. The best of Lopez's work occurs on that thin border where the two approaches meet. As is the case with many a writer, it has taken Lopez some years and several books to find the balance between reality and imagination, to hew the unmarked line and discover his forte. This is true to a great extent because of his journalistic background and the innate difficulties involved with his chosen subject, the relationships between post-industrial man and primitive nature. On the last score, it is somewhat of a conundrum to considser what one might say about nature that already hasn't been said by the variously sinewy, softheaded, and occasionally brilliant members of the band of nature writers. Surely we already know that "God made the

8

country, man made the town." All else would seem elaboration on an old theme.

Barry Lopez's father was a Spaniard born in England. His mother's family dates far back to immigrants arriving in Pennsylvania in the 1670s. Born in 1945 in Port Chester, New York, Barry spent his early years on the other end of the continent, in the rural San Fernando Valley of California. He remembers his life among "alfalfa fields, sheep, and horses. Trips into the Santa Monica Mountains, to Malibu Beach. Mesmerized by the Mojave Desert, summers at Grand Canyon and at Arrowhead Lake" (Letter from Lopez, 20 December 1982). At the age of eleven, he moved with his family back across the continent to Manhattan. Following graduation from the Jesuit high school, he attended the University of Notre Dame. After studying history, English, and drama, he graduated cum laude and worked for the better part of a year as a sales representative for New American Library. He subsequently married, completed a Master of Arts in Teaching at his alma mater, then studied journalism and folklore at the University of Oregon, in Eugene.

But the figure now hailed on the college lecture circuit never taught full time. Lopez was still grappling to gain his professional feet. In 1970, at the age of twenty-five, he followed his intuitions and settled in Finn Rock, Oregon, an unincorporated logging village set among the peaks of the Cascade Range. There he continues to live with his wife Sandy, while making—another item for the list of dualisms—periodic lecture forays to Eastern cities and journeys with naturalists to the Alaskan Arctic.

Lopez looks back with appreciation for the disciplined but broad intellectual grounding offered by his years of academic studies, which included heavy doses of Latin, French, and mathematics. He comments: "I depend a good deal on my formal education and return to it as often as I return to the woods, which is to say daily" (Letter from Lopez, 20 December 1982). The reference to the outdoors points to a parallel, nonacademic schooling taking place in Lopez's youth. While still in his teens, for instance, Lopez worked two summers on a ranch near Moose, Wyoming. Here he performed the unromantic chores that make up much of ranch life, digging innumerable holes for innumerable fence posts, clearing trails, packing equipment and supplies to mountain camps. Similarly, while attending Notre Dame, he often visited with friends in the hilly farming country of West Virginia. During such periods he was absorbing the landscape, which was becoming a focus for his life, which was leading him off on camping trips into the Western United States and Canada.

He traveled mentally as well as physically. One summer in Wyoming the cum laude spent many a night in the bunkhouse entertaining himself by translating the polished tropes of Vergil's *Aeneid* into modern-day English. That represents something of the measure of the man. Not that ranch life bored the undergraduate with a liking for Latin. While putting muscle on his frame, Lopez was assimilating the outdoors and developing a keen respect for his fellow ranch hands, the unschooled but sensitive men who lived closely with nature on a day-to-day, demanding basis. The experiences would serve him well as material. Out of them grew "Dave's Story: Five Dollar Dogs," a piece that avoids sentimentalizing either man or coyote while capturing the pathos in the harsh life of a bounty hunter, and "Grown Men," which eulogizes country people, secure in what they are doing while leading "obscure and exemplary lives" (p. 19) in harmony with their natural surroundings.

What emerges, then, is a picture of Barry Lopez as a well-educated, somewhat withdrawing but affable person with his antennae fixed on the natural world. Personal qualities overlap with professional interests, for it is a dual portrait in which the concerns of Lopez the man and Lopez the writer correspond:

> I care about language and landscape, both separately and for the connection between them, which is what writing is to me. I think a great deal about the therapeutic value of story and language, and about the ethical issues in writing. I once said I wrote because of a hatred of lies. And that I went into the natural world because you could examine the nature of your prejudices there without fear of reprisal.
>
> The issues that concern me most—for which natural history has been the metaphor I am most at home with— are the nature of prejudice; the play of compassion in human life; and the place of awe and mystery in adult life. (Letter from Lopez, 20 December 1982)

This seems a straightforward enough credo and explanation of a writer's task. Certainly it echoes many of the values assumed in a long humanistic tradition that gives dignity to man and honors his capacity for intellectual exploration. But in the familiarity, the familiarity recognized and readily praised by the reviewers, lies a problem. Is Lopez speaking of absolute values, or is he, perhaps unwittingly, mirroring romantic cultural prejudices? Are language and landscape essentially connected? Is writing art or is it therapy? Do ethics and esthetics necessarily go together? Can a truth teller be a creator of mysteries? Does Lopez, along with a host of other writers in our European tradition, correctly assume that truth lies embedded in nature, a precious metal awaiting extraction?

With such questions we approach the crux of Lopez's work, for Lopez the dualist attempts to be both reporter and poet. He began, it should be remembered, as a journalist—essentially an urban calling—a reporter of the natural world, and the impulse remains strong. Yet at the other pole, the poet in him, the creature of the romantic imagination exploring nature, has tugged demandingly at the writer, insisting that reportage is not enough.

To simplify somewhat, in his later volumes—*Of Wolves and Men* and *Winter Count*—the two forces work in graceful syncretism. Before he achieved the balance, we see in his earlier works—*Desert Notes, Giving Birth to Thunder*, and *River Notes*—that the journalist and the poet do not always complement each other harmoniously and convincingly. Rather, they compete for stylistic prominence, and at times they stand wholly apart in the same volume. Lopez's first book, the fictional *Desert Notes*, consists of eleven brief chapters. In general, they concern one man's encounter with facts and fables in the deserts of the American West. This much, then, unifies them. But in the approaches to the subjects, at times it seems that two authors are writing the book.

At one extreme stands "The School" (pp. 61-66). Here, an unnamed female narrator takes the journalist on a visit to the country schoolhouse of her childhood. As have abandoned buildings everywhere across the United States, it has been vandalized, doors and windows torn out by curiosity seekers, the interior and exterior blasted with shotguns and rifles. "All these holes scattered in the walls are from hunters," notes the former pupil. "They come by looking for coyotes and rabbits and shoot at this because it's the only thing around" (p. 61). As the two visitors step over the debris, the woman points to the broken glass, feces, and the remains of a fire started in a corner. Then, in contrast to the violated building, she begins to re-create the school as she remembers it from the 1920s. Here were the fine double oak doors, there Miss Lamse's exquisite teak table, a treasure brought from far-off San Francisco to grace the country school. The narrator recalls the details that haunt her from childhood: the handle that warmed in the slant of the afternoon sun, the bell tolling recess, the pattern in the grain across the highly polished hardwood floors. She giggles remembering the time the children were busy waxing their desks "to look nice for Christmas" and, at a scream, all ran to the cloakroom to see five dead rats hung up as a prank by one of the erumpent boys (p. 64).

Lopez has passed on more than the record of a sentimental journey. The old school was a focus for the rural people, something sacred and shared in their hard lives, a symbol of the community's pride, one now senselessly defiled by uncaring outsiders. "The School" is one of the most convincing pieces in *Desert Notes* because, though doubtlessly the speaker is cut by the pain of loss, she describes the school, both past and present, matter-of-factly, journalistically. The pain is implied, though strongly felt by the reader. In this tension lies the power of the piece.

At the other end of the spectrum Lopez offers "Perimeter" (pp. 37-41). The author takes us on another visit, this time to a rather strange landscape in the arid West, an area of blue mountains with gray creeks that make "a terrific noise." These unusual watercourses apparently enjoy lives of their own, for they have the habit of changing their beds every three or four years (p. 37).

That is the frame for the "story," its location. The rest is elaboration. Lopez describes the region's vegetation, caves, and wildlife. The features have peculiar attributes. "The smells include the hellebore, vallo weed and punchen; each plant puts out its own smell and together they make a sort of pillow that floats a few feet off the ground where they are not as likely to be torn up by the wind" (pp. 37-38). The water in caves "smells like oranges but has no taste" (p. 40). Lopez points to a herd of twelve buckskin horses. We can hear their footsteps from ten miles away. Among the chokecherry bushes lives a dog of such importance or insignificance that he receives the one-sentence paragraph: "An old tawny long-haired dog lives here" (p. 39).

One wonders what to make of "Perimeter," except that it is an unfinished piece of writing spun off from a freewheeling imagination. Its details are interesting, sometimes arresting, but they lack coherence. As does the inept science-fiction writer, Lopez has attempted to create an aura of mystery by indulging his hallucinatory impulses, turning them loose on nature and following his whims. The results are complicated but not complex. They neither convince nor move with the authority of the well-crafted "The School." The chapter ends abruptly, without preparation, the excurrent catalog arbitrarily chopped off with the hardly credible pronouncement to the reader that now "You know where everything is coming from" (p. 41).

Both impulses, the journalistic and the imaginative, come together in "Twilight" (pp. 25-33). Stylistically and thematically the piece divides neatly into two parts, the separation emphasized by extra space between the dividing paragraphs. The subject is a Navajo rug. In the first section, Lopez assumes the guise of the investigative reporter. He makes up the history of the blanket beginning with its theft from a grocery store in Winslow, Arizona, in 1936 by a down-and-out farmer. It changes hands several times, traveling from California to Wisconsin to Florida. Along the way, the purchasers treat the rug as a valuable curiosity rather than as an objet d'art. Each time the rug is sold, the owner inflates its pedigree to sound more glamorous and revises the price upward. Finally, the errant rug ends its peregrinations when the author purchases it.

The realistic technique is intriguing. Where will the writer take the story? How will he get out of the corner into which he has painted himself?

He simply spreads his imaginative wings and flies out of it. He goes out into the desert and crawls around on the rug until he begins having visions: "Already I have seen the priest with his Bible bound in wolves' fur and the blackbirds asleep in his hair" (p. 28). The fanciful scenes change rapidly:

> This is the only time you will see the turtles massed on the eastern border for the march to the western edge where there is water, and then back the same night to hide in the bushes and smash insects dazed to lethargy in the cold. I have spoken with these turtles. They are reticent about their commitments. Each one looks like half the earth. (p. 31)

In any case, the message entails contrasting attitudes toward a Native American artifact. Clearly, the series of crass owners has viewed the rug as a commodity, in terms of potential dollars. On the other hand, the "I" of the story would tell us he truly appreciates it as a vehicle to the mystical world of the primitive. This is a risk-filled area for an Anglo writer to enter. We know of Lopez's respect for American Indian thought, which he studied at the University of Oregon. Since then he has enlarged on that background and drawn deeply from it for his writing, for instance editing "The American Indian Mind" issue for *Quest* magazine. The poet W. B. Yeats indeed asserted that primitive peoples "live always on the edges of vision" (*Essays and Introductions* [New York: Collier Books, 1961], p. 42). However, the sense of artistic "rightness" we often get from Indian mythology is not readily captured by a white person's attempt to create "instant" mystical awareness. Lopez's visionary "trips" on the blanket in "Twilight" are flashy but glib. They smack of the magic carpet theme of childhood fantasies. One does not simply "get in tune" with a Navajo rug and therefore break the bounds of technological civilization for spiritual flights into a culture enriched by centuries of struggles with nature. The idea would appall, if not insult, a traditional Navajo. And finally, as with "Perimeter," "Twilight" ends without justification, without a sense of artistic form. The author simply lops off the visionary catalog by wrapping himself up in the rug and going to sleep (p. 33).

In 1977, Barry Lopez further pursued his interests in Native American lore by following *Desert Notes* with *Giving Birth to Thunder, Sleeping with His Daughter: Coyote Builds North America*. The humorous title points to what comes after, an anthology of Indian tales about Coyote, the trickster figure of many tribes. The sixty-eight stories are ribald, surreal, lighthearted, sometimes homiletic: "Coyote Imitates Mountain Lion," "Coyote's Member Keeps Talking," and "Coyote Gets His Head Stuck in an Elk Skull." In one incident, which brings to mind Walt Disney's cartoon character, feisty but impetuous Coyote has his dinner disturbed by the noise of two trees rubbing together in the wind. The hot-blooded little wolf climbs up into the trees to settle the matter and of course manages to get himself pinned between the offending branches. Thus suspended, he must suffer the additional humiliation of watching other animals gather below to eat his meal (pp. 55-56). But Coyote isn't always the bumbling clown. In another episode he plays the role of mythic benefactor by first bringing fire to people (pp. 11-14). In still another, the most ghostly and complexly satisfying piece in the collection, Coyote restores a dead Indian girl to life, only to allow her to die again when her father abuses him (pp. 26-28). If the reader is looking for several evenings of alternately easy-going and haunting entertainment, *Giving Birth to Thunder* surely will provide it.

But not much more. Lois Wickstrom gushed in the *Rocky Mountain News* about Lopez's masterful rendering of the tales into idiomatic English ("Coyote Tales Inspire Retelling," 12 March

1978), and in this respect Lopez deserves credit for a job well done, but the effusion typifies reviewers' quick trigger fingers for praise. In fact, American Indians might well be miffed by the book's dedication to them. Serious students of Native American literature might follow suit. Lopez rewrote archival material to fit his own purposes, a circumstance he speedily admits in his introduction (p. xviii). In the process, however, he steamrolled through a good many subtleties of Indian mythology. Some of the original tales have Rabbit, Mink, and Raven for their main characters. Lopez changed them into Coyote at his convenience. His rewriting streamlines the stories, leaving out incremental repetitions and number patterns important to their native contexts. He thus slights the traditions which provide the settings for Native American storytelling. For instance, in some tribes a particular tale may be told only after the first frost, while in another a story may be recounted no more than once a season by an individual. In the foreword to *Giving Birth to Thunder*, noted folklorist Barre Toelken somewhat surprisingly sweeps such issues aside with, "It does *not* pretend to be an 'Indian book'" (p. xiii). In response, one might quite logically ask, "Then what kind of a book *does* it pretend to be?" Not content with Toelken's offhand disclaimer, Dell H. Hymes refuses to let such matters rest and on their account gives the collection a switching: "... you may value having English versions of so many [tales] from such a range. You may be troubled, though, and if you are of Native American descent, you may be dismayed" (Review of *Giving Birth to Thunder*, p. 91). Wherever the matter eventually rests, one might wish that Lopez's journalistic rectitude had come more to the fore during the conceptualization of the project. As it stands, the collection offers a pleasant but not enlightening excursion into American Indian lore.

Two years after *Giving Birth to Thunder*, reviewers greeted *River*

Notes as "a work of genius" containing "an abundance of rewards and revelations" (David Miller, "A Sense of Harmony," p. 59; and Harry Mark Petrakis, "A Poet Seeks the Life Force in Dark Waters," p. 3). Whereas *Desert Notes* focussed on brief excursions into the West's arid places, Lopez's third book concentrates on water imagery. Whatever the implications of the change in scene, the reader of *River Notes* finds himself in familiar territory regarding structure, style, and underlying message. The predominant "I" of the short chapters visits riverine places instead of deserts, and though the author's revelations are not as hallucinogenic as in his first volume, the intent is much the same: to report back to his audience on mystical experiences gained through the medium of nature.

The first piece, "The Search for the Heron" (pp. 3-9), sets the tone of spiritual search for the following vignettes. On a rainy day mirroring the mood of the author, he is watching a heron. As he follows the bird along a river, he speaks to it as an embodiment of primitive forces in a visionary world: "I know: your way is to be inscrutable. When pressed you leave. This is no more unexpected or mysterious than that you give birth to shadows. Or Silence" (p. 3). As he skulks along, catching glimpses of the bird moving ahead through the bushes, the man ruminates on his spiritual prey, imagining its various attributes: "Your sigh, I am told, is like the sound of rain driven against tower bells. You smell like wild ginger. When you lift your foot from the river, water doesn't run off it to spoil the transparent surface of the shallows. The water hesitates to offend you" (p. 4). The toplofty heron keeps hopping ahead of him, and the maple trees refuse to give the human enquirer any information. However, the cottonwoods oblige by telling of the heron's own dreams of dancing in an assembly of "more than a hundred great blue herons riveted by the light of dawn" (p. 5).

After a while, the author gives the reader some indication of the reasons for his strange searches. He has been wounded, but he leaves the agents of his debility obscured in veils of romantic vagueness: "I have been crippled by my age, by what I have known, as well as by my youth, by what I have yet to learn, in all these inquiries" (p. 8).

Finally, as often occurs in Lopez's work, the piece ends with an attempt at epiphany. The author gathers some of the bird's fallen feathers and sleeps on them. He has "a great dream." The heron stands before him resplendent and instructs him about the beginning of the world. The man awakes and an "unpronounceable forgiveness" sweeps over him (pp. 8-9).

Not all the chapters that follow are as pat or as insistently visionary. One reports on the apparent drowning of several boatmen ("The Rapids," pp. 51-55). "The Salmon" (pp. 59-65) concerns a distraught individual, "mired in the swamp of his thought" (p. 61), who builds a great stone fish in a river. A third, "Drought" (pp. 95-100), is the account of an enervating dry spell. It is brought on, like some scourge on stiff-necked Egyptians, because "no one remembers how to live anymore" (p. 99).

As in *Desert Notes*, *River Notes* sparkles here and there with arresting details. Pursuing the heron in the first chapter, Lopez the spiritual voyeur of nature spies the bird standing "before a terrified chorus of young alders" (p. 3), a literary treat for the reader. And to describe the troubled young man in "The Salmon" who earnestly scribbles in his journal and then abandons it "as though leaping from a small airplane" (p. 62) is to describe a troubled young man indeed. Still, the pleasant surprises of such passages may point to a promising talent, but they do not, as occasional as they are, make a successful book. As was the case with *Desert Notes*, almost all of the pieces in *River Notes* again play off—with little further development—the central theme: in contrast to our current technological civilization, physical and spiritual well-being springs from getting in tune with nature. One might quite agree with Lopez's premise vis-à-vis the essential worth of nature but disagree with certain major aspects in his presentation.

Perceiving themselves as locked in technological labyrinths, people need to dream of things, if not better, then at least more mysterious than their present condition. Hence, in an age shadowed by the possibility of intercontinental nuclear war, a time of computerized bank tellers and lobotomized television programming, we also have astrologers, palmists, and a growing number of religious cults. As Peter Steinhart says, writing of Bigfoot and the Loch Ness Monster, whether or not these two creatures exist is not the substantive issue. Rather, "Mystery is itself a human need. The imminence of discovery is as essential as sunlight or sleep. If the narrowing monotony of modern life denies us a sense of impending discovery, we will take it out in dream and hysteria" ("Hidden Animals," *Audubon*, January 1983, p. 12). Lopez writes in a time of growing ecological awareness, in a period when for many readers a more primitive life seems to offer an alternative, an escape from a souring, industrialized dead end. He has, then, as have writers on various themes throughout the ages, struck a popular cord. That in itself of course is not a denial of a writer's worth, witness examples from Euripides to Márquez. But despite their immediate popularity with readers and reviewers, had his first three books done more than satisfy transient enthusiasms? Had he broken through to new territory and written enduringly about it? Had he, in short, transcended the clichés of his time?

Perhaps not. David Quammen, a novelist from Montana, is one of the few evaluators who has assayed Lopez's work through other than popular eyes. While praising his later writing as "fine, informative," "pared down and elemental," he refers to *River Notes* as "a disappointing collection of pretentions" (Review of *Winter Count*, p. 14). Not that Lopez is engaged in a deliberate public deception. Rather, despite his earnest efforts, his early books fail to present a convincing whole for other than undiscriminating readers. The case rests on two related aspects of his work.

The first is a difficulty already discussed. He can't seem to command his journalistic and poetic instincts to pull in a cooperative effort and bring reality and imagination into a common, believable focus. The second concerns a spectrum of literary "sins" often found in unrefined romanticism. These stem essentially from oversimplification, from a will to euphoria based on little more than wish fulfillment. Already noted is Lopez's romantization of the American Indian, his falling into the trap of the myth of the "noble savage." Close to this is the assumption that contact with nature is an antidote to civilization's ills. It may be for some people, especially in small doses. But to a large extent Lopez glosses over the harsher aspects of nature, the madness and starvation that greeted many a pioneer who plunged off into the wilderness neither forewarned nor forearmed. Even gentle Tennyson, in gentle England, acknowledged that nature can be "red in tooth and claw." Be that as it may, we might grant that under certain controlled circumstances exposure to the wilds can be therapeutic, that days spent alone in the wilderness can relieve our assaulted senses, before our return to the comforts of civilization. Yet the problem for the writer, whatever his position in this regard, is to tell us more than we already know or believe.

In addition, Lopez's facile presentation of the "back to nature" theme often leaves us suspicious of the speedy efficacy of the cures and of his quick flights into realms beyond ordinary life. "Dawn" (*River Notes*, pp. 79-83), for instance, offers a sensuous view of a

21

young woman disaffected with life in general, and with her husband in particular, undergoing such therapy. While her mate sleeps up at the house, she walks down to a nearby river. She fantasizes about an osprey telling her stories. She lies naked in the water, then climbs out:

> She sat down on the rock in the print dress, the sunlight prickling with the coolness of the river over her and feeling the movement of air over the rock. She dried her eyes with the hem of the dress and saw in the island of hair between her legs suspended—she was overcome with tenderness—two small bits of alder leaf, bright green. (p. 83)

Though one may not deny her very real sense of temporary well-being, she thus joins the cast of Lopez characters who through sliding into waters or meditating on desert ledges gives us not insights into their human complexities but recitations of cliches. Opposed to them but no more satisfying are those who, lying on a Navajo rug or talking to trees, undergo improbable flights which the writer fails to make believable. Either way, whether through the predictable or the unlikely, he has created pseudo-mystery, not mystery.

River Notes appeared in 1979, but Barry Lopez had been working simultaneously on another book, which appeared a year earlier. In light of the three works already discussed, the changes in this fourth volume come as a surprise to the reader working through the Lopez oeuvre. The *Times Literary Supplement* called *Of Wolves and Men* a "replevin," an attempt to rescue the wolf from its maligned, centuries-old image (Matilda Traherne, Review of *Of Wolves and Men*, p. 102). The author himself spoke of it in terms of "rejuvenation," not only of man's understanding of a persecuted animal but of a more sensitive approach to natural surroundings (Lisa

Connolly, "The Man Who Cries Wolf as a Center of Creation," p. 3). Both estimates are correct. However, added to them, *Of Wolves and Men* is a rescuing of the author's very prose.

In his earlier works, Lopez indulged himself in earnest but unconvincing psychic tours, and at first thought the encyclopedic approach of *Of Wolves and Men* might make it, too, appear diffuse. But *Canis lupus* grounds the book, forces the writer to confront a difficult subject and make demands on his abilities. As the animal appears first up close as an object of science, then flickers variously through history, mythology, and philosophy, it provides the writer with the focus for his sights lacking in previous volumes. The ambitious study of the wolf from several perspectives makes a book which enlightens the reader while testing the best of its writer's realistic and imaginative talents, bringing them, once at odds, into a satisfying whole. *Of Wolves and Men* is Barry Lopez's watershed.

In accepting the Nobel Prize in 1954, Ernest Hemingway mentioned the value of just such a demanding situation, one driving the writer "far out past where he can go, out to where no one can help him," as essential for producing enduring literature (*Nobel Prize Library* [New York: Helvetica Press, 1971], p. 7). That Lopez—or any other man for that matter—was beyond his depth with the subject of wolves is axiomatic. On the one hand, many cultures including our own have evolved wolf mythologies, mythologies riddled with misconceptions but taken as fact about the feared creature. On the other, Lopez notes with some incredulity that in a nation proud of its scientific accomplishments "the first unbiased ecological treatise" on the animal was not published until 1944 (*Of Wolves and Men*, p. 224). A near hiatus followed until a flurry of wolf studies beginning in the 1960s strove to rescue knowledge of a persecuted animal on the verge of disappearing from the contiguous United States (pp. 223-24). On top of that, the wolf—

few in numbers, highly mobile, requiring a vast territory, fearful of man, often nocturnal—is not an easy creature to observe. And until the recent growth of environmental concerns, legislative bodies were loath to appropriate money for studying a beast thought to be the enemy of children and cattle, an animal deemed better dead than alive.

Lopez, untrained as a scientist, added further difficulties to the matter. He admired science but felt it incapable of making ultimate pronouncements about wolves or men. Science measures, it assumes that the reality of the wolf or of anything else can be reduced to numerical data. Lopez would not be so easily satisfied. He knew that wolves can find trails through the sensitive pads of their feet, that they share food and give gifts. He had observed wolves in Alaska, individuals with puzzling tics and quirks, with eccentricities and changeable moods similar to those of human individuals. From the specific to the general, he dug through dusty tomes and watched the wolf "loping along with that bicycling gait, through all of human history, appraised by all sorts of men but uttering itself not a word" (p. 206).

As a result of such ponderings, several things suggested themselves to Lopez. Though science offers a helpful tool to understanding the wolf, it is not the only tool. In this sense, science is simple in its linear logic, while reality is complex and organic. Lopez speculates about the possibility that wolf behavior changes over time. If it does, this "means that social animals evolve, that what you learn today may not apply tomorrow, that in striving to create a generalized static animal you have lost the real, dynamic animal" (p. 81). The wolf, either individually or as a species, is not "reducible" to a computer printout (p. 204). The scientific method, then, tends to look for something that does not exist, for "The mistake that is made . . . is to think that there is an ultimate wolf reality to be divined, one that can only be unearthed with microscope and radio collar. Some wolf biologists are possessed of the idea of binding the wolf up in 'statistically significant' data. They want no question about the wolf not to have an answer" (p. 80). That is not, hastens the author, "to damn [scientific] knowledge." It is only to say that neither "men nor machines . . . can be described entirely in terms of endocrine secretions and neural impulses. Like us, [wolves] are genetically variable, and both the species and the individual are capable of unprecedented behavior." Science offers only a tool, one that, as valuable as it is, cannot "by itself produce the animal entire" (p. 284).

With that, the author seems to have reached an intellectual cul-de-sac. He finds a way out of it with the observation that among the Nunamiut Eskimos "The animal is observed as a part of the universe." In other words, our view of the wolf should be multiple, just as reality itself is multiple (p. 80). Lopez's purpose is to take the "wider view" of the wolf in its variously changing contexts in time and place (p. 284).

That would be a difficult enough task for any author in any one volume, but, pursuing his own questionings, Lopez takes on yet another burden. Pondering man's changing attitudes toward the wolf in different cultures over the ages, he concludes that wolves, as with all phenomena, are as much products of the imagination as they are of science. "We create wolves," he pronounces bluntly (p. 203), and he goes on to assert more generally that "it is the imagination that gives shape to the universe" (p. 285). He elaborates: "Biologists turn to data. Eskimos and Indians accept natural explanations but also take a wider view, that some things are inexplicable except through the metaphorical language of legend" (p. 2). Thus his study considers "fact" and imagination as inextricably related. As with all valid ecological writing, it deals with interrelationships. *Of Wolves and Men*, founded on the premise that men have created varying concepts of wolves, tells perhaps more about the human psyche than it does about the physical wolf loping along in isolation through the centuries. As the introduction summarizes, "The truth is we know little about the wolf. What we know a good deal more about is what we imagine the wolf to be" (p. 3).

From such a stance, the author could plunge easily into a vague romanticism, but the organization and reasoning of Lopez's study, unlike features found in volumes previously mentioned, is clear-cut, lucid. Following the pattern of the above speculations, the book begins with a summary of scientific information, then moves on to an opposing section, the wolf as perceived by Native Americans. The third part, again contrasting sharply with the latter section, recapitulates the pathological mania for slaughtering wolves throughout the brief history of the United States. The book concludes with a compendium of the wolf in European folklore. Though one might wonder a bit why the author did not follow a more chronological plan, in any case the reader has no difficulty knowing where he is in *Of Wolves and Men* or what it is the author is saying.

He also knows that *Of Wolves and Men* is a polemic, though a gentle one, designed to persuade him toward a more sympathetic view of the wolf and untrammeled nature. Lopez accomplishes this, not through wild-eyed tours of fantastic landscapes or hallucinogenic flights on Indian rugs, but through the presentation of his scholarship on the subject coupled with moderate nudges questioning the destructive role of industrialized societies. No doubt, the biologist specializing in *lupus* will not be especially enlightened by Lopez's first section. For example, it begins by describing one of the book's subjects: "The wolf weighs ninety-four pounds and stands thirty inches at the shoulder. His feet are enormous, leaving prints in the mud along a creek (where he pauses to hunt crayfish but not with much interest) more than five inches long by just over four wide. He has two fractured ribs, broken by a moose a year before. They are healed now, but a sharp eye would notice the irregularity" (p. 10). But at this point at least Lopez's purpose is not to impress zoologists. Rather he is engaging the general reader. Working against Little-Red-Riding-Hood prejudices of the wolf as a ravenous enemy of humankind, he presents the animal as an individual, like all creatures including man, constantly adjusting to the web of nature, a creature of beauty, stamina, and keen adaptability. Lopez takes his readers to a wolf den. He reveals a wolf body language based on eye movements, "Nose pushing, jaw wrestling, cheek rubbing, and facial licking" (p. 47). He shows wolves chasing ducks, seemingly for the sheer joy of it, or, jaws snapping, seriously pursuing a moose.

The author takes few pains to hide his admiration for his subject, but though his passages can be alternately lyrical and realistically descriptive, they remain within the province of scientific truth. For instance, the portrait of pups in their den, leading to the implications of the closing sentence:

> After the pups are weaned, the other members of the pack play an increasingly greater role in their upbringing, providing both food and recreation. The pups eat partially digested food regurgitated for them by adults. Babysitting adults play rag doll to the pups, who now have needle-sharp milk teeth and are mobbing each other, wrestling, biting, and generally grabbing reclining adults vigorously by the ruff of the neck. This behavior will later be molded into efficient hunting technique. (p. 35)

By dehumanizing their victims, by stereotyping them, totalitarian governments ease their way into persecutions, much as civilizations have stereotyped wolves and persecuted them almost to extinction. Taking the opposite tack, Lopez brings the reader into the particularized world of individual wolves, a complex world where "more is going on than we understand" (p. 57). Ticking off various subspecies, such as Japanese, Newfoundland, and Texas wolves, all exterminated or hard-pressed, Lopez suggests that a mystery is slipping through the world's fingers: "By whatever standard, a significant part of the genetic reservoir that once represented one of the more adaptive mammals on the face of the earth is now gone" (p. 15). Thus, informing his readers, stirring them with appreciation and a sense of loss, Lopez skillfully prepares them for deeper conceptual changes in the chapters to follow.

Having shown his animal and gained rapport with his audience, the writer dives into a dimension in which the wolf is "both substance and shadow" (p. 78), the sphere of Native Americans where the physical and mythological intermix. It is a realm that few biologists, trusting to their "facts," have entered. The contrast is immediate, for this multilateral region requires "a different understanding" if it is to be perceived (p. 79). Whereas the white scientist arrives in the field by helicopter or motorboat to stay a few weeks, at best for a few months, he is not at home there, physically or psychically. He depends on technological support from a civilized base. In a sense, he arrives armed with limitations, for he sees what his education has prepared him to find, what his equipment can measure. In Lopez's way of looking at it, this avenue to his subject violates the very essence of ecology. It is not integrated with the surroundings.

Opposed to the scientist's detachment, some traditional Native Americans and wolves share the same topography, blizzards, and droughts. In this sense, the Indian is more like the wolf than the scientist. Furthermore, in the case of some Eskimos, the human hunters depend on the same food, the caribou, as the wolf eats. In such circumstances, both man and wolf deal with similar conditions for survival. The biological lesson concerning nature "red in tooth and claw" is clear to Eskimo and wolf alike: kill caribou or die.

Because of this, traditional Native Americans went beyond admiring wolves for their hunting abilities to imitating their hunting skills. Lopez works his way through the details of the resulting cultural ramifications. He recounts the various roles of the wolf in Indian mythologies, reprints an Indian wolf song, and includes a discussion of wolf warrior societies (pp. 114-34). All this information, interesting as it is in itself, he presents to support his main thesis, again one in conflict with the attitudes of whites and their wolf-fearing, wolf-killing tradition: "The Indian was so well integrated in his environment that his motivation was almost hidden; his lifeway was as mysterious to white men as the wolf's" (p. 105). Given the environment of interlocking details, to understand the wolf we must understand the Indian, and vice-versa. Lopez illustrates:

> What, if anything, does this correspondence mean? I think it can mean almost everything if you are trying to fathom wolves.
>
> It became clear to me one evening in a single question.
>
> An old Nunamiut man was asked who, at the end of his life, knew more about the mountains and foothills of the Brooks Range near Anaktuvuk, an old man or an old wolf? Where and when to hunt, how to survive in a blizzard or a year when the caribou didn't come? After a pause the man said, "The same. They know the same." (p. 86)

All other lessons of *Of Wolves and Men* spring from this central unity. Though its occurrence early in the book makes what follows anticlimactic, the remaining sections bear their own related historical dramas and revelations of the human psyche. Part III, "The Beast of Waste and Desolation," is a literary charnel house documenting man's inhumanity to wolves as one aspect of his abuse to his home planet. But here we are dealing with more than the usual destruction, intended or not, that man has visited on his environment, for he has pursued the wolf with a manic intensity that other animals have escaped. Ranchers assumed that *lupus* was a bloodthirsty stock killer and shot, trapped, and poisoned him almost off the face of the United States. The federal government, yielding to political pressure, joined in the attack, spending millions of dollars on the frenzied slaughter.

Cattlemen, as wrongheaded as they may have been, at least had an excuse for their enmity. But why, asks Lopez, would men with no apparent self-interest at stake kill wolves with a near religious intensity, with, as he puts it, an "almost pathological dedication" (p. 139)? Because, he goes on, the "hatred has religious roots; the wolf was the Devil in disguise" (p. 140). In psychological terms, throughout the centuries Western man, unlike the Native American, has felt uncomfortable with wild nature. Not living intimately in it, not understanding it, he has hated it:

> In the Bible, wilderness is defined as the place without God—a sere and barren desert. This twined sense of wilderness as a place innately dangerous and godless was something that attached itself, inevitably, to the wolf—the most feared denizen of gloomy wilderness. As civilized man matured and came to measure his own progress by his subjugation of the wilderness . . . the act of killing wolves became a symbolic act, a way to lash out

> at that enormous, inchoate obstacle: wilderness. Man
> demonstrated his own prodigious strength as well as his
> allegiance to God by killing wolves. (p. 141)

The wilderness that to the American Indian was home, a sacred place wherever he wandered, threatened Europeans, who projected their fears onto the wolf, a psychological twist explored in greater detail by other students of history, notably Lynn White, Jr. ("The Historical Roots of Our Ecologic Crisis," *Science*, 10 March 1967, pp. 1203-07) and Roderick Nash (*Wilderness and the American Mind*, 3rd. ed. [New Haven, Connecticut: Yale University Press, 1982]).

With *Of Wolves and Men* Barry Lopez accomplished what he set out to do. He informed his readers and moved many of them to reevaluate their cultural prejudices, with the end that some day perhaps the society as a whole could "find some way to look the animal in the face again" (p. 199). The book marks a strong development in Lopez's writing. In *Of Wolves and Men* we find almost none of the flimflams of vague pseudo-mystery that plague his earlier work. Instead, the writer concentrates on the particular. He applies an imagination guided by a keen sense of journalism, bringing it to bear on his concerns for Native American ways and environmental issues.

It is a mature, controlled, and inspired work, and this time reviewers praised not the volume's faddish appeal but Lopez's smooth and persuasive handling of intricate arguments. Matilda Traherne commended it as an erudite but lyrical "mirror to superstition" (Review of *Of Wolves and Men*, p. 102). Noting the book's artful blend of natural history, psychology, and folklore, *Newsweek* helped win *Of Wolves and Men* a wide audience by recommending it as a "fresh, original work" (Walter Clemons, "Howl," p. 112). With greater literary dexterity, Eve Auchincloss illuminated Lopez's balance of journalism and imagination as "poetic precision." She continued: "In this soft-spoken, haunting meditation of wolf and man, Barry Lopez tries to show what we have lost and why" ("The Beauty of a Beast," p. 4).

Whatever the large measure of justified praise, some periodicals became stormy in their enthusiasm and blustered on in ways that one might guess embarrassed its author. *The New Yorker* labeled the study "near-comprehensive" (Review of *Of Wolves and Men*, p. 122), while *The Christian Science Monitor*, seemingly in competition for superlatives, did the magazine one better by declaring Lopez's analysis "exhaustive" (Diana Loercher, "Man vs. Wolf: Who Is the Beast?" p. 3). Another critic, a noted zoologist who should have known better, dropped discretion and crowned Lopez with "something new—a bridge between books of the past and those of the future" (George B. Schaller, Review of *Of Wolves and Men*, p. 34).

As if anticipating such excesses, *Of Wolves and Men* repeatedly warns against the arrogance of anyone claiming an "exhaustive" study of the wolf (pp. 2, 3, 4, 57, 78, 81, 97, 203, 270). Far from laying any claims to uniqueness, the text gives careful credit to other scholars of the wolf, such as David Mech, Farley Mowat, Adolph Murie, and Robert Stephenson. In the same year as the publication of his wolf volume, Lopez paid homage to scientists Michael W. Fox, John Lilly, and Joan McIntyre, who had preceded him in spanning the gulf between animals and human perceptions of them ("Where the Wild Things Are," p. 85).

Perhaps far more revealing than the popular reviews, with their competition in encomiums for a book climbing on the sales lists, were the well-tempered reactions of professional biologists. Lopez, after all, was an admitted amateur challenging the scientific status quo with unconventional theses. While seeking out a few soft places—Christen Wemmer rightly zoomed in on the "pure corn" of an anthropomorphic passage or two—the reviewer from the National Zoological Park blessed the author for a "fine historical perspective" created through a "scholar's eye." Wemmer's favorable judgment reflected the opinions of colleagues (Review of *Of Wolves and Men*, pp. 194-95; see also Rita Campon, "Wolves," p. 101; and Robert Pilsworth, Review of *Of Wolves and Men*, p. 122).

Lopez's *Of Wolves and Men* explores possibilities beyond the narrow realm of how traditional science perceives animals. Speculative as it is in parts, the book is not fiction. It is a study of how humans see and understand. *Giving Birth to Thunder* similarly is nonfiction. Though Lopez may be faulted by some scholars for changing specific details of Indian myths for his own unifying purposes, in the main it is an anthropological collection, pretending no credit for the creation of the stories. *Desert Notes* and *River Notes*, however, arc fiction, for they attempt to create new realities by restructuring experience. As indicated, they fall short of the mark by offering exaggerations that fail to convince. In contrast, *Winter Count* transcends the traps of the two previous fictive works and leads the reader into worlds of credible wonder.

Taken as a whole, the raison d'être of Lopez's work is to re-create a sense of mystery supposedly lost by our technological civilization. He does this by pointedly reminding that "It is, after all, not man but the universe that is subtle" (*Of Wolves and Men*, p. 97). Lopez wants to bring his readers into a soul-sustaining intimacy with nature. While maintaining the purpose, *Winter Count* succeeds where his earlier fictional attempts foundered. Here he abandons jejune romanticism with its abrupt escapes and facile, exhilarative leaps into the primitive. In its place he constructs intellectual, finely wrought exaltations. Like Daniel Defoe in *Robinson Crusoe* or *Journal of the Plague Year*—but for quite different ends—he constructs a careful structure seamlessly blending elements of fact and imagination.   Into this he places, not the flat if frenetic characters of earlier books, but people who while anchored in quotidian reality are trying to surpass it, to escape into mystery.

The escape can be permanent in a special way but only for individuals willing to pay a price which would discourage most people. Through sacrifice, through focussing their lives, a few of the characters in *Winter Count* have crossed over into extraordinary worlds. But first, through discipline and self-imposed limitations, they have made themselves psychically sleek for the passage through the eye of the needle.   However, it is the nature of romanticism that most of its adherents will not pass through entirely. They will catch glimpses only and be tantalized by the few evanescent moments that show them the realm of possibilities. The nine short pieces in *Winter Count*, then, deal with two kinds of romantics, the priests and the aspirants. Taken together, the two groups stand apart from the far more numerous bourgeois society that surrounds and often oppresses them. With such a schema, *Winter Count* introduces a landscape of tensions and complexities.

The title of the book reflects the author's continuing fixation on transcendental events and his philosophic dedication to the redemptive qualities of Native American ways. Certain Plains tribes marked the passage of a year by embodying it in a notable event.   Represented pictographically on an animal skin, the sequence is known as a "winter count." Metaphorically, the individual pieces in the book are psychic highlights. Yet, again differing from *Desert Notes* and *River Notes*, the "I" of the stories often is all but submerged—and when he does appear to play an active role it is not of a fire-breathing, levitated narrator but of the humble neophyte still in the process of learning, a process, we are given to understand, which he and several other characters may never complete.

"Restoration" (pp. 3-14), the first piece in *Winter Count*, illustrates the above concerns and serves as a paradigm for much that follows. As in most of the story plots, events unfold quietly. Their significance is implied, understated, as if readers were hearing a leitmotif softly played in the background. Lopez uses this technique so skillfully that even when later on in the volume extraordinary things happen—when a herd of ghost buffalo appear or when stones rise from the ground and fly about—we are awed rather than suspicious.

In "Restoration," the "I" is driving east into North Dakota from Montana in 1974 when a billboard catches his eye: "Killdeer—HISTORIC FRENCH CHATEAU • 12 MILES • ICE CREAM • COOL DRINKS • SOUVENIRS" (*Winter Count*, p. 5). As does many a tourist ready for a break from the weary miles, the narrator stops. He takes a tour of a mansion sitting outside town on the undulating prairie, which "gives the impression . . . of being a military outpost on the edge of an empire of silence and space" (p. 4). A pamphlet informs him that the anomaly was built in 1863 by a noble French family, the de Crenirs from Bordeaux. Apparently, the de Crenirs used the "chateau" as a rather lavish wilderness summer home. However, the last person to use it, René de Crenir, became fascinated by the still wild surroundings and lived there year-round for seven years. He left inexplicably in 1894. Now a local historical group is refurbishing the property.

On his tour, Lopez strikes up a conversation with one of the employees. Edward Seraut is performing the delicate task of restoring René de Crenir's book collection, which includes the classic volumes of travel and zoology of the day. The two men go out for dinner. The rest of the story concerns their brief relationship and the author's attempt to probe de Crenir's mind through deciphering the notes that the Frenchman made in his books. While that hardly is a gripping plot in the normal sense of the word, the intellectual and emotional impact of Lopez's short stay at the mansion leaves the young man reeling. Here, as in other stories, we meet the novice, the romantic aspirant suddenly confronted by spiritual crises that leave him shaken and confused, sometimes exhilarated, by the possibilities glimpsed.

Unlike Lopez's previous fiction, the circumstances in which the mental welter develops often can be common enough, with little out of the ordinary perceived by characters in the book not attuned to subtleties. The "chateau" after all is chock-full of ordinary tourists. And one might indeed follow in Lopez's steps to find the town and the mansion he describes. One might walk along with a group of tourists similar to the one Lopez mentions, noticing bored young girls with fingers sticky from melting ice cream. However, there will not be a Seraut restoring books, because he is created by the author. Hence, the slip from historicity into imagination goes entirely unnoticed and rings entirely true.

Nonetheless, Seraut is essential to Lopez's purposes. He acts as a foil for the romantic neophyte "I" of the story, who first sees him "sitting still and jacketless in a straight chair with a broken book in his lap, as though bereaved" (p. 5). Like other priest figures in *Winter Count*, Seraut stands apart, veiled in private mystery. Lopez's implications in this regard are far more important than the few bits of solid information revealed about the man. He is cultured and reserved, with a tinge of the European lingering about him, an outsider in Killdeer, North Dakota, esthetically devoted to a craft which few tourists or townspeople appreciate. Furthermore, he bears an aura of suffering, as if rebuffed by the world he prefers to dwell in isolation within the rich bittersweet kingdom of his reveries. Such a characterization might come off as fey and sentimentalized, but Lopez keeps the man sharply in focus with an

36

alert journalistic eye for the details that themselves create the man. His manners suggest "polite intentions and cultivated tastes," and the precision of Seraut's tools makes them appear "surgical" (pp. 7, 6). When, with the assistance of after-dinner wine and cigars, he finally drops his reserve, his description of his craft marks him with the "passion of the art and obscurity of his profession" (p. 8). Lopez himself uses religious imagery, for there is something of "the air of a prior" about this well-read but reticent gentleman in his sixties (p. 7). He is just the figure to stir the romantic yearnings of the young visitor to the de Crenir mansion with its aura of screened mystery.

Dualisms nest in "Restoration" like Chinese boxes. The surrounding environment isolates the esthetes in two ways. To the two new acquaintances, Killdeer is a bastion of Yahooism, not a place to exercise one's sensibilities. The restoration of the mansion may be laudable in itself, but it is funded through the claptrap hype of the garish billboard welcoming visitors to the community. While the younger man sits after dinner absorbing Seraut's "atmosphere of ideas and history," he is disgusted by "young, ferine men cruising in slow-moving pickups on the other side of the window, or distracted by the rise and fall of ranchers' voices and the din of country-and-western music in an adjoining bar" (p. 10). The older gentleman, subjected to the stares of tourists while he mends books but hardened to the crassness of the crowd, handles the embarrassment differently while in purgatorial Killdeer. He withdraws into himself and avoids contact with the hoi polloi. The narrator, however, young, in a state of newly awakened awareness, is pained by the discrepancy.

Secondly, the landscape of brown sweeps dotted by antelope also isolates the two men, but their reactions to it are dissimilar. Seraut has all but cut himself off from intrusions into his narrow sphere of mental safety. "I've been here for months," he tells the young man toploftily, "and I've hardly looked out the windows" (p. 5). From what little is known of him, René de Crenir also withdrew from many normal contacts, and it is the anomaly of the mansion's cultured but hidden past impinging on the wild plains that sets the neophyte's imagination afire. What was de Crenir doing here on the "empire of silence and space" (p. 4), sitting year after year among his collection of extraordinary books? The possibilities tantalize the narrator, because he presupposes a dramatic answer that may not exist. Indeed, the mystery may exist only in this young tourist's mind.

Yet, if a romantic search for elusive intangibles is not easily gratified, it also is not easily stymied. Part of the ironic humor of the narrator's quest is his credulous assumption that he can fathom de Crenir's mind in the few days allotted to him in Kildeer. Reading through the Frenchman's marginalia, he is startled to find that the foreigner, working alone, concluded that the American Indians based their philosophy on the ways of animals—thus anticipating an idea current in modern anthropology (p. 12). The discovery rattles the narrator in disproportion to its historical significance. For the point is not that a visiting tourist unearths a tidbit from history, but that a young man runs into concepts that feed his enthusiasms and further propel him into a pattern leading to frustration.

For his part, Seraut encourages the research "in a genial way" that disguises a deeper wisdom (p. 13). Seraut understands, in a way that the researcher, wrapped in his naive enthusiasm, cannot, that the excesses of youth lead to suffering. Confronted with the information about de Crenir, Seraut turns the protégé's attention to a book he is mending. The narrator doesn't perceive what is going on: "When I hesitated to hold it because of its beauty," he wonders in retrospect, "he urged me to take it, to listen to the rattle of its pages, to examine the retooling" (p. 12). Unlike the young man, Seraut knows his limitations and has adjusted his expectations to an inconstant world of promises. No rushing hither and yon after speculations for him. Whatever his refinement, his defense against uncertainty is tangible, the day-to-day ballast of restoring valuable books. In the midst of intellectual misgivings, it is the one factor he can control. It is his anchor. In contrast, emotional ups and downs typify the youthful romantic searcher, and as the realization of the situation begins to dawn on the young man, he gloomily considers his own notes avidly taken, now "the black ink like a skittering of shore birds over the white sheets" (p. 13).

In the wider view of Lopez's writing, then, he has toned down his romanticism, enriching it and making it credible by bringing it in line with realities, or, better stated, by butting it against realities. That is not to say that he has abandoned dealing with ineffable moments—only that he does so more convincingly. Now the epiphany is not heralded in dramatic banners but treasured or suffered in the narrator's heart. In some ways, "The Lover of Words" (pp. 89-97) is the reverse of "Restoration," for here the written word eventually does bring solace. But not before it administers a large dose of pain. The truth that the main figure seeks will make him free, but first it will make him miserable. He is a Mexican gardener in Los Angeles. Little distinguishes him from other men of his station, except that he enjoys spending his free time reading to a degree that is "sublime and pervasive" (p. 89). However, despite the sloganeering of librarians, books are not always friends. Accompanying his daily enjoyment comes the growing recognition of his limited personal circumstances. In this state of lost innocence, discontent gnaws at him in proportion to the extent that he nourishes himself with words. Between the two, he is a torn man. For a time, the gardener beats himself against the surrounding walls of reality, then exhausted by the inner turmoil, he accepts his situation, thinks "of the inscrutable life buried in a wheelbarrow full of bulbs," and reads on (p. 97).

In one sense, this is a retreat, but again, as in the case of Seraut, a retreat can be a gain of sorts if it is into the fortress of a newly recognized and newly valued self. Seraut's wide-eyed aspirant has just begun the process of the antagonists in *Winter Count* who, tried in the fires of frustrated aspirations and doubt, emerge glowing with their own versions of hard gem-like flames. As with the Mexican gardener, it can be an ennobling hedonism, this discovery of self as a palace of art. Quiet, subtle, internalized, often it occurs as a blessing bestowed by nature—the gift of a seashell or the ephemeral glimpse of a flock of birds that take on transcendental significance borne away in the heart.

Perhaps nothing better represents the change in Lopez's approach than a comparison of the garishness of "The Search for the Heron" (pp. 3-9) in *River Notes* with "Winter Herons" (pp. 17-25 of *Winter Count*). Rather than the megalomanic cosmic voyeur pursuing a bird clumsily cloaked in mythical garb, here we meet a man sitting on a marble bench in the midst of rush-hour New York City. While he waits for his girlfriend, the story takes place as a series of reflections. As with almost all of Lopez's characters, he must pass through crises to his epiphany. Like the Mexican gardener, he, too, is torn. He is attracted to his lover, but she is too citified to enjoy his treks into the wilderness. He feels agony over the death of his father. He is chafed by the discord of civilization on the streets around him. Then he remembers an evening some time back when he was strolling home late one evening in a snowstorm and stopped abruptly in his tracks:

> He had walked only a few blocks when he realized that
> birds were falling. Great blue herons were descending
> slowly against the braking of their wings, their ebony

legs extended to test the depth of the snow which lay in a garden that divided the avenue . . . . After a moment they were all still. They gazed at the front of a hotel, where someone had just gone through a revolving door . . . and a flapping suddenly erupted among them and they were in the air again. Fifteen or twenty, flying past with heavy, hushing beats, north up the avenue for two or three blocks before they broke through the plane of light and disappeared. (p. 24)

As it fits into the man's conflicts, the phenomenon remembered is more personally reassuring than ornithologically miraculous. As we have seen, with *Winter Count* Lopez has shifted his attention from the dramatic blare of large events to the significance of small ones.

The attempt to glean transcendental experiences from such evanescent circumstances sometimes goes awry. "Winter Count 1973: Geese, They Flew Over in a Storm" (pp. 53-63) yet again presents the redemption-through-birds theme. While an adequate job of writing, it does not compare well with the previous moment of relief brought about when an unexpected flight passes through the consciousness of the main character. Even Lopez's admirable prose cannot rescue the pat situation. An aging professor well-known in his field attends a conference in New Orleans to deliver a paper on the topic of winter counts. Yet he is wearied of conferences, wearied of the depersonalized milieu of big cities in general and of such gatherings in particular. His ennui grows as he perceives the dichotomy between his artificial surroundings and the primitive ways, the natural adjustments to nature by Native Americans, that are the focus of his life's study. He is a man who "long ago lost touch with the definitive, the awful distance of reason" (p. 61).

After his talk, as gloomy as ever, he goes back up to his hotel room, throws up the window to the rain, and hears "In the deepest distance, once . . . , the barking-dog sounds of geese, running like horses before a prairie thunderstorm" (p. 63). Perhaps we can grant that "God made the country, man made the town," but the professor comes across not so much as an esthetician but as a cranky old man, shot through with self-pity and unappreciative of his colleagues. One need not be a devotee either of big cities or of scholarly assemblies to expect that, whatever the causes of the professor's malaise, he would be just as dismal sitting in a Sioux lodge as he is in a New Orleans hotel room. He may think that the call of wild geese can redeem him, but it is instead a false anodyne and, further, a justification for the self-indulgent lingering over his own vague sorrowing.

Elsewhere, the narrating "I" appreciates the esthetics of seashells. "A form of genuflection turned over in the hand becomes a form of containment, its thin pastels the colors to chalk a prairie sunrise," he muses with the sensitivity that will break his heart. The description is inimitable, but again not worthy of what follows. The man next buries himself at dusk on the sand of a Caribbean beach and waits to be spiritually overcome. We are almost back in the world of *Desert Notes*. He hears his pulse drowned out as the thousands of shells around him begin "a wailing, a keening as disarming, as real, as sudden high winds at sea." Then an attractive woman appears. Unaware of the narrator, she begins picking up shells with "cranelike movements" (p. 80). For his part, the young man wants to call out to her, but, struck to the heart by the gestalt of the situation, he is paralyzed: "My respect for her was without reason and profound. I lay for hours unable to move" (p. 81).

As unlikely as this sounds, a string of unlikely coincidences follows as "The Woman Who Had Shells" (pp. 79-86) develops. The man later spots her in a restaurant in New York City, where the two talk "about bumblebees and Cartier-Bresson, haiku, Tibet, and Western novels" (p. 83). They go to her apartment, where they sip tea and continue the eclectic discourse through the night to the twilight hours. At last, as a special favor, she grants him a look at her collection of seashells. Like the woman, they hold mystery, for they are so delicate he can "see the color of my skin through them" (p. 85). At this juncture the reader is ready for a physical romance finally to commence, but after a moment of silence, the narrator plods out into the dawn, still plagued by a "fundamental anguish," of what source the reader doesn't know, though one assumes that it is generated by the combination of the lady and her shells (p. 86). Again, one might appreciate the diaphanous sentiments and wish that such a platonic tryst happened, or at least could happen, but there can be a vast difference between sentiment expressed by a character and sentiment felt by the reader. In "The Woman Who Had Shells," the former appears as the product of schwarmerei, of a factitious romanticism on the part of the author. Lopez has violated the boundaries of the plausible.

Sometimes, in contrast to the everyday circumstances of "Restoration," "The Lover of Words," or "Winter Herons," he also can overstep the bounds of what we normally would consider reality—and get away with it by producing his own brand of subtle magic. In "Buffalo" (pp. 29-35), for instance, Lopez becomes the literary magician who deftly leaves us pleasantly amazed.

Skillfully disarming the reader, he does this by laying a supposed historical basis for the piece, as he did in "Restoration." Again, when the break occurs, the reader is so convinced that he is not aware of his smooth levitation out of history and into imagination. By then, anything seems possible. In "Buffalo," Lopez assumes the guise of a professor carefully retelling a puzzling event and trying to fit its pieces into a logical whole. This much he knows: in January of

1845, a party of Cheyenne hunters camped in a river bottom. But the winter takes a bad turn, as it often does on the high northern plains. After a thaw, freezing weather moves in, creating a dangerous crust on the snow cover. This is a trap for a nearby herd of buffalo. When the animals attempt to move, they break through the brittle surface, slashing their legs on the broken ice. All around the little camp of the Cheyenne the creatures "lay scattered like black boulders over the blinding white of the prairie, connected by a thin cross-hatching of bloody red trails" (p. 30). The death moanings go on through days and nights, rattling the Indians. As soon as the weather permits, the terrified Cheyenne leave.

The professor continues putting together the information. After the carnage, he informs us, buffalo never again inhabited the location (p. 31). And there are other strange details scattered in old records. As the hunters were departing hastily for home, one of the party reported seeing a small group of buffalo leaving the plains, headed toward the mountains. They were all white and larger than any buffalo he had ever seen (p. 30). The professor also unearths the fact that a Shoshoni Indian called Long Otter climbed into the range and discovered a huge white herd among the peaks. On his approach they began singing a death song (p. 32). Several tribes in the area have speculated about the meaning of this. To add to the mystery, some Arapaho also climbed the mountain and found the buffalo, which began chanting as before and then floated away ghost-like through the clouds. The Arapaho concluded that the buffalo had foreseen the coming of the white men. The animals were trying to warn the Indians and show them a way to escape the coming destruction of their culture by leaving through the sky (p. 34).

In terms of reality, where are we: in the realm of history or folklore? One can believe certain of the details as factually true and put down others to the fears of superstitious Stone Age peoples. So most white readers would react at this point in the story. And so Lopez, understanding this, is manipulating readers for what follows. As it turns out, the professor continues, scientists writing in the *Journal of Mammalogy* have discovered the bones of buffalo on the peaks of the mountains mentioned, of an unusual size and at altitudes not normally expected. The skeptical reader checking the references the author provides will find the material essentially as presented in "Buffalo." Might the Indians have been correct in their interpretation? The European mind tends to keep fact and fiction separate, but here Lopez weaves them together to leave us bewildered, doubting our previous, matter-of-fact realities, leaving us open to possibilities we had not expected.

This is both the message and the accomplishment of Barry Lopez's best works. *Of Wolves and Men* and *Winter Count*, one a factual study with speculative overtones, the other fiction, are closely related, for both attempt to shake the reader out of his normal perceptions. Both books dare him to consider wider potentials in interpreting the world he is passing through. As Dyan Zaslowsky summarizes Lopez's assimilations of science and magic, "The stories in *Winter Count* are a deft and fragile synthesis of the real and the impossible, and all are endowed with the authority of history, yet each with an authenticity that defies proof" ("In Indian Way, These Tales Blend Real, Impossible," p. 21).

It has been a long and not a smooth process for Lopez himself. The author gained his writing legs with articles in *Popular Science* which instructed subscribers how to fell trees. He next plunged into a period of glib romanticism. Most importantly, however, he moved beyond this easy plight to the far more difficult task of disturbing while elevating the reader's sensibilities, of in a sense setting the reader in a challenge against himself. As the Mexican gardener in

"The Lover of Words" discovered, this can be a discomforting experience, though one necessary to growth. Accomplishing this is a measure of any writer's worth.

Selected Bibliography

MATERIAL BY LOPEZ

"The American Indian Mind." Barry Lopez, ed. *Quest*, 2 (September-October 1978), 109-24.

"Borders." *Blair & Ketchum's Country Journal*, 8 (September 1981), 32, 34-36.

"The Bull Rider." *Chouteau Review*, 2 (Spring 1978), 53-62.

"Children in the Woods." *Pacific Northwest*, 16 (April 1982), 8.

"Dave's Story: Five Dollar Dogs." *North American Review*, 264 (Spring 1979), 52-53.

Desert Notes: Reflections in the Eye of a Raven. Kansas City, Kansas: Sheed, Andrews and McMeel, 1976.

Desert Reservation. Poetry chapbook. Port Townsend, Washington: Copper Canyon Press, 1980.

"A Faint Light on the Northern Edge." *North American Review*, 267 (March 1982), 12-21.

Giving Birth to Thunder, Sleeping with His Daughter: Coyote Builds North America. Kansas City, Kansas: Sheed, Andrews and McMeel, 1977.

"Going Down with the Bulls." *North American Review*, 259 (Summer 1974), 3-7.

"Grown Men." *Notre Dame Magazine*, 8 (October 1979), 17-19.

"In a Country of Light, among Animals." *Outside*, 6 (June-July 1981), 36-45.

"In Little Things I Find the Cosmos." *National Wildlife*, 11 (February-March 1973), 42-47.

"In Search of Silence." *Travel & Leisure*, 7 (November 1977), 81-82.

"Laying It on the Line." *Running*, 6 (November-December 1981), 42-48.

"The Lives of Seals: Reflections on Killing Animals in the Name of Science." *Science*, 3 (November 1982), 50-55.

"Mighty Chickadee." *National Wildlife*, 13 (April-May 1975), 32-33.

"Murder: A Memoir." *Rocky Mountain Magazine*, 3 (May-June 1981), 58, 60.

"My Horse." *North American Review*, 260 (Summer 1975), 8-10.

Of Wolves and Men. New York: Charles Scribner's Sons, 1978.

"One for the Heart." *Running*, 9 (January-February 1983), 34-39.

River Notes: The Dance of Herons. Kansas City, Kansas: Andrews and McMeel, 1979.

"Searching for Ancestors: An Interrogation of the Landscape of the Anasazi." *Outside*, 8 (April 1983), 74-77, 84-86.

"Weekend." *Audubon*, 75 (July 1973), 62-67.

"Where the Wild Things Are." Book reviews of *The Cult of the Wild*, by Boyce Rensberger, and *Thinking Animals*, by Paul Shepard. *Harper's*, 256 (February 1978), 84-86, 90.

Winter Count. New York: Charles Scribner's Sons, 1981.

WORKS ABOUT LOPEZ

Auchincloss, Eve. "The Beauty of a Beast." Review of *Of Wolves and Men*. *Chicago Tribune*, 5 November 1978, Sec. 7, p. 4.

Backes, Clarus. "A Beer with a Writer of Feeling." *Denver Post*, 19 April 1981, Sec. R., p. 23.

Campon, Rita. Review of *Of Wolves and Men*. *Natural History*, 90 (February 1981), 101.

Cheuse, Alan. Review of *Winter Count*. *Saturday Review*, 8 (April 1981), 78.

Clemons, Walter. "Howl." Review of *Of Wolves and Men*. *Newsweek*, 16 October 1978, p. 112.

Connolly, Lisa. "The Man Who Cries Wolf as a Center of Creation." *Los Angeles Times*, 15 July 1979, Books Sec., p. 3.

Hymes, Dell H. Review of *Giving Birth to Thunder, Sleeping with his Daughter: Coyote Builds North America*. *Western Humanities Review*, 33 (Winter 1979), 91-94.

Kendall, Elaine. "Literary Pictographs as Slides of Life." Review of *Winter Count*. *Los Angeles Times*, 9 April 1981, Sec. 5, p. 28.

Loercher, Diana. "Man vs. Wolf: Who Is the Beast?" Review of *Of Wolves and Men*. *Christian Science Monitor*, 12 February 1979, Sec. B., p. 3.

Miller, David. "A Sense of Harmony." Review of *River Notes: The Dance of Herons*. *Progressive*, 44 (April 1980), 58-59.

Petrakis, Harry Mark. "A Poet Seeks the Life Force in Dark Waters." Review of *River Notes: The Dance of Herons*. *Chicago Tribune*, 25 November 1979, Sec. 7, p. 3.

Pilsworth, Robert. Review of *Of Wolves and Men*. *New Scientist*, 12 July 1979, p. 122.

Quammen, David. Review of *Winter Count*. *New York Times Book Review*, 14 June 1981, pp. 14, 18.

Review of *Of Wolves and Men*. *The New Yorker*, 26 February 1979, pp. 122-23.

Review of *Winter Count*. *Virginia Quarterly Review*, 57 (Autumn 1981), 137.

Schaller, George B. Review of *Of Wolves and Men*. *Animal Kingdom*, 82 (April-May 1979), 34.

Traherne, Matilda. Review of *Of Wolves and Men*. *Times Literary Supplement*, 7 December 1979, p. 102.

Webster, Bayard. "A Bad Press." Review of *Of Wolves and Men*. *New York Times Book Review*, 19 November 1978, p. 44.

Wemmer, Christen. Review of *Of Wolves and Men*. *Smithsonian*, 9 (November 1978), 194-195.

Zaslowsky, Dyan. "In Indian Way, These Tales Blend Real, Impossible." Review of *Winter Count*. *Denver Post*, 19 April 1981, Sec. R., p. 21.